MW01194284

HOW TO PLAN YOUR CELEBRATION OF LIFE

...WHILE YOU STILL HAVE A SAY

Brenda Coonan

How to Plan Your Celebration of Life ...While You Still Have a Say

©2018 Brenda Coonan

ISBN: 978-1-999-39621-3

All rights reserved. No part of this book may be used or reproduced by any means graphic, electronic, or mechanical including printing & photocopying, recording, taping, or by any information storage retrieval system without the written permission of the publisher except in the case of brief quotations embodied in critical articles and reviews.

Illustrations by Author

Cover Designed by CREATIVE ARTZ

NOTE: Any links and brand names used here were not paid for and no benefit accrued to the author for using them. They are not to be interpreted as a promotion of a website or product, just references relevant to the content of this book.

Contents

How to Plan Your Celebration of Life... While You Still
Have a Say   1

Before You Begin: Know Thyself   3

Key Considerations   5

Time to Get Started   9

    Attendees   *11*

    Speakers   *19*

    Where will your Ceremony of Life be held?   *21*

    When?   *23*

    Activities   *23*

    Food & Refreshments   *25*

    Music   *27*

Congratulations, You've Got Your Plan ...   29

Notes   31

How to Plan Your Celebration of Life... While You Still Have a Say

You didn't have much control over your entrance into this world, but with a little planning you can take control of your exit.

If you were to be hit by the proverbial bus today, what would your loved ones know about your final wishes? Your proudest moment? Your most cherished accomplishments? The words you were planning to say? What impression would you want to leave the world?

Have you ever attended a memorial service for a friend, and thought maybe you had wandered into the wrong place? A pin-drop quiet atmosphere, a somber crowd; the total antithesis of someone best remembered for getting wallflowers to try anything once? If a spirit can have regrets, it is likely that your friend was spinning.

Whether we choose to ignore it or not, we are all going to die. Thanks to life's curve balls, we're rarely given a heads-up on the precise timing.

Whether you envision leaving this world with a bang, or slipping gently into that good night, documenting your intentions is key.

A 'good bye' doesn't have to be complex, but mapping out an exit plan ahead of time, helps to ensure that wishes will be honored when you can no longer speak for yourself. By providing clear directives, you are gifting your loved ones with a final act of kindness, not burdening them with organizing an event when they are least emotionally prepared to do so.

Friends and family will be comforted knowing that by following your plan, as simple or as bizarre as you choose to make it, you will have left life on your terms.

By thinking of others during your planning, you'll also be adding some last-minute brownie points to your personal legacy. And, who can't use more of those?

Planning your Celebration of Life early will enable you to fine-tune it with important details as the memories come to you. Remember Mom's *mind-numbing* peanut butter squares? Those magical concoctions that mollified all your childhood traumas? With a little planning, those squares can spread their magic once again, featured front and center on a buffet table.

Whether you set aside a weekend to work out the particulars of an elaborate scavenger hunt, or continually add detail to a 10 minute plan roughed out on a napkin, the sooner you have things down in writing, the sooner you will have lightened the load for both you and those left behind.

The following pages can help you to decide the direction you'd like to take.

They may also tweak a memory or two.

BEFORE YOU BEGIN: KNOW THYSELF

How would you like to be remembered? Be honest here. Are you more of a good book in front of the fireplace person, or are you always itching to dress up and meet people in the latest hotspot? There is no right answer. It's okay to be a book-loving-fireplace-hugging-hermit who always longed to dress up and hang with beautiful people. This is your final hurrah and you can choose to make your exit any way you like.

It may be a bit of a stretch to expect the city to shut down upon your demise, but even quiet people can arrange to go out with a significant bang. It just takes a little planning.

You aren't an overpaid movie star, this is your life. You don't get another take. Unless science announces some pretty incredible discovery, you are not going to be 'undead' anytime soon.

Write your own ending. No one can tell you you're wrong.

What do YOU want?

Do you want your Celebration of Life to be in addition to, or combined with, a more traditional funeral service?

For practical reasons involving the reality of decomposition, traditional services generally follow very closely after death. Increasingly however, people are choosing to extend the time between death and the Celebration of Life. The extension allows immediate family and friends the time to mourn as unabashedly and intensely as needed. It can also provide for a more controlled and memorable experience later, when acquaintances that were less directly connected or challenged by factors such as distance, can join the event. With emotions more in check, and time to adjust to a new reality, mourners are generally better organized and equipped to recall and appreciate the experiences being shared.

Your Choice

For the purposes of this book, we will focus on the Celebration of Life as being its own entity, separate from the more immediate funeral ceremony, burial, or cremation details. What you choose to include, combine, or skip altogether is totally up to you.

Your "Last" First!

This is your life's 'last' first. It's big! It is the only time you (or your loved one, if you are planning for someone else) will make this exit. There are no ground rules for you, and no mandate to follow a standard template designed around societal norms. Consider modifying traditional, contemporary, and personal preferences, to make your event more representative of your life.

KEY CONSIDERATIONS

What is important to you?

Are there important beliefs that you want incorporated into the occasion? Hidden talents that you've been saving for a big reveal? Do you want people who influenced you, or that held a special place in your heart, recognized?

Is this ceremony going to be your final 15 minutes of fame?

Think about how you want to be remembered.

Who do you want to attend?

The initial list of people you would like notified, should be flexible. Listing by categories like family, friends, acquaintances, colleagues, and neighbors, makes it easier to adjust the list as you go. The earlier you create your list, the more people will come and go from your life.

Set a reminder to review your list on a regular basis. Pair it with your annual health checkup and celebrate! You'll have one more year under your belt and a list of people to be thankful for, or to potentially add to the "maybe" list.

What is your budget?

Once you have decided on the type of service, the  approximate number of people that you expect to attend, and the basics of the ceremony, you can work on determining how much you would like, or are willing to spend.

Establishing a budget early helps to focus the planning and ensures that the key aspects are taken care of first. Extras and "nice-to-haves" can be tacked on after you have the important aspects down in writing. Remember to allow for inflation and changes in your own financial status.

Whether you decide to talk to your financial planner, insurance company or banker, determine where the funds for your event will be kept. Don't leave family and friends in a state of confusion about this important aspect of your plan.

Avoid paying for any arrangements too far in advance. Your ideas can fluctuate, and venues and service providers can change hands or go out of business. Read the fine print and ensure you are covered in case of such events.

Safeguard Your Wishes.

Designate a person, persons, or entity to be responsible for safeguarding and executing your written plan. This can be a friend, family member, or lawyer's office. A backup is always a good idea.

Avoid potential for miscommunication by clarifying your plans as much as possible. While a simple ceremony may infer a casual backyard bbq to you, others may interpret "simple" to mean a parade of past, barely remembered acquaintances at a "simple" black-tie affair. It is easy for people to default to their own biases when left without sufficient instruction.

While it may initially make people uncomfortable, sitting down with family and friends to discuss Celebration of Life planning *before* that 'bus' rounds the corner, can be highly beneficial. Not only does it provide an opportunity for you to let people know how important they are to you, but it can allow others to provide valuable input. Details that you may never have thought of can become part of your ceremony. You can also explain the reasoning behind decisions that may have seemed unclear or out of character for you.

Don't count on having time, or all of your faculties, to clarify details at the end. Remember those curve balls?

Time to Get Started

There is no right and wrong way to start your plan. The key is to *begin*.

Who? What? WHY?? When?? HOW?

Designate a notebook or file to hold all the information. Computers are great, but if you are opting to use one for planning, ensure that someone knows where to find your document and any associated passwords when the time comes.

Planning centers around answering the questions: who, what, why, when, where, and how. It doesn't matter in what order you choose to answer the questions. You can fill in missing details later.

Consider using the following basic questions as starter headlines to help clarify the end goal on your initial skeletal plan. A few sample responses have been included.

● Why am I having a Celebration of Life?
   ○ Answering this question will set the tone for the rest of your planning.

- ■ To ensure those deserving recognition receive it
- ■ To avoid an overly sanctimonious ceremony
- ■ One last party
- ● Why is it important to plan ahead of time?
  - ■ It removes the burden of responsibility from the shoulders of friends and family
  - ■ It helps me visualize how I want to be remembered and can act as a lodestar
- ● Who will attend?
  - ○ Family
  - ○ Close friends
  - ○ Church and club associates
- ● Who will be responsible for guarding, overseeing and executing my plan?
  - ○ My lawyer will hold the instructions
  - ○ Youngest sibling and best friend will share duties
- ● What will the ceremony look like?
  - ○ My '65 Ford Mustang Fastback will be parked in front of the venue
  - ○ Photos of family, friends, church and club members will be displayed everywhere
  - ○ Favorite music from 50's will play around bonfire at old homestead
- ● When the time comes, when will the ceremony be held relative to my demise?
  - ○ It will follow shortly after cremation
- ● Where will it be held?
  - ○ Town's event center and family acreage

- How will it be accomplished logistically and financially?
  - ○ Will work with insurance agents, banks, lawyers, family members, and different services and facilities to coordinate and align needs

The initial questions always spawn more and more questions. Those responses lead to the details that make your ceremony unique to you.

Below you will find some other aspects to consider and suggestions that will help you to expand your basic plan.

???

Attendees

The number of people can be trimmed down or added to later if necessary, but for now, get the list started. The number and the relationship of the people attending will help to determine the location, mood, and timing of your event.

Who would you *like* to be there?

If there are people that are MUST-ATTENDS, ensure that you allow them the time and, if necessary or desired, any financial assistance that they may require to be there.

Remember, dividing attendees up into categories helps to tweak the memory and assist with planning. Considering using indicators like 't' *for travel time*; '$' *for financial assistance* and 'v' for *video/facetime attendance*, to mark attendees that may require extra consideration.

Who won't be invited?

If you will rest easier knowing that the neighbor who kicked your dog won't be attending, put him on the "definite no" list. You don't have to endure people who spoil the vibe. This is your final hurrah. Final moments should be shared with those you truly care about. "No Dog Kickers" signs are subtle and humorous, yet effective.

_____

_____

_____

_____

_____

How will potential attendees find out about the ceremony of life?

- Arrange a phone chain. Have one person from each category of attendees responsible for contacting others in their category. Responsibility can be shared down the line.

- Pre-record your own intro message to play at the appropriate time. Say you are sorry that you can't attend but you will be there in spirit! Provide any basics of the ceremony that you can and point them in the direction of where they can get more information.

- Arrange for a hand-delivered notice.

- Make an announcement. Arrange for any trade, volunteer group, or organization that you once belonged to be notified.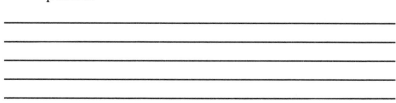

- Take out a newspaper or radio ad. Maybe you always wanted to make the pages of the New York Times? Now is your time.

- Have you got a social media account like FaceBook, LinkedIn or Twitter? Share your access codes with someone you trust and have your 'goodbye' notice posted.

What will they wear?

If you want attendees to dress in your team colors or in clown costumes, it is within your power to ask. Likewise, a request to refrain from large hats or perfume is not too much to ask.

_____

_____

_____

_____

Identify Guests

Name tags that identify attendees and how they are connected are thoughtful additions. Use tags that don't ruin clothing. Have them available as guests arrive.

Everyone has heard about Uncle Leo, the bank robber. Let them put a face to the name!

Getting people to add their nicknames or AKAs to the tags can add to camaraderie among the guests When you've referred to your best pal as 'Snake' your whole life, identifying them only as 'Jeeves' or 'Christina' on the nametag, will leave people wondering just how good a friend this 'no show' Snake really was.

Transportation

Depending upon logistics, organizing group transportation to and from venues could help build camaraderie or improve the flow of the day. It's a great accompaniment to an event where alcohol is served.

_____

_____

Video and written messages

It is rare, in this day of international travel and habitation, that everyone will be able to make it. Allocate time for video Facetimes and the reading of written acknowledgements from those unable to attend. Don't forget to make a special note to contact these out-of-towners in a timely manner.

Do you need assistance in arranging this? Who could help you find a vide-ographer?

_____

_____

A photo table

Photo tables can rarely be too big. Displaying photos of family and friends, both predeceased and alive, can help to explain important relationships and resemblances. They can also break the ice with guests who can help each other out by explaining relationships to each other.

Who could help you gather and organize photos?

_____

_____

Shake Things Up?

Did you always want to have a standup comedian at your final show? A local celebrity? A team mascot? A live band? Go for it! Most people will love it and you won't get another chance.

Who could help you source entertainment?

_____

_____

Separate ceremonies.

If you've spent significant portions of your life in different parts of the country, or even around the world, you probably developed meaningful relationships in many locales.

In situations where it is not feasible for separate groups of people to travel to a central location, duplicate or simultaneous remote ceremonies may be warranted. Today's technology can be of great assistance with both live feed and recordings.

Professional video production companies, or many twelve-year-old children, can help in this area.

Who? What? Where? Time Zones? Travel? Video? Lots to consider.

_____
_____
_____
_____

Pets are people too?

If you treat your pets like family, don't neglect to include them. If they will be going to a new home, consider including the passing of the ownership within the ceremony.

Don't forget to put someone in charge of scoop bags if Fido is present. He may want to mark the occasion in his own way.

_____

_____

_____

Who will be in charge or oversee the event?

Religious or cultural affiliations can make choosing someone to oversee the event easier. More and more people, however, are soliciting this service from friends or non-denominational officiants. While choosing "personality appropriate" friends and family to oversee a variety of duties is becoming more popular, it is still prudent to have one chief organizer or event planner in charge of the day. Too many cooks truly can - unintentionally - spoil the broth.

_____

_____

_____

Speakers

Who should speak at the event?

How about starting with you? It is your last chance to make a final impression. You can start by making an audio or video recording that you can continually update with thoughts you may want to share.

Some sentiments that you may want to include:

- It's basic, but don't neglect to thank people for coming.
- Tell people how special they are. Use specifics as much as possible: Make it personal. "I would never have won the Nobel Peace Prize without the triple shot mochaccinos from *Fred's Fuming Java*."
- Advise attendees where you are donating your favourite musical instruments, or paintings, so that they can continue to enjoy them.

- Tell them your spirit plans to be at the corner of King & Main on Fridays at 3pm if they ever need to talk.
- Tell your favourite corny jokes.
- Apologize *only* for those things that may warrant a "sorry about that."
- Tell people to remember the good times, to relax, and to mingle.
- Remind attendees to tell their loved ones how they feel about them. Life is short.
- Have a bowl of suggested good deeds that people who choose to, can draw from. They can remember

your connection when they continue to make the world a better place.

_____

_____

_____

Tips For Speakers

- Choose speakers carefully among family and friends. Not everyone wants the duty. Ask them ahead of time if you need to be sure.

- Make a note to ensure that the sound system works and that those speaking are shown how to talk into the mic properly. It can be frustrating when the back of the room can't hear.

- Begin speeches early in the program to avoid too-tipsy raconteurs.

- It can be surprising how many people like to get behind a microphone when given the chance. Setting a limit on the number of speakers, and the time allotted to each, helps to ensure that guests remember you, not the celebration that dragged on ... and on ... and on.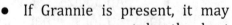

- If Grannie is present, it may not be the best  time for your Mongolian prison tale. If there are other life stories that you prefer were left off of the agenda, make your wishes clear ahead of time. Remember, you can take some secrets with you.

- Arrange for a guest speaker, surprise or otherwise. The choice is totally up to you but leaving your guests wondering about the speaker's relevance to your life may not be the result you were hoping for. Put some thought into your choice.
- Monitor speakers. Have someone in charge who can tactfully remove a speaker if necessary. Everyone knows that Uncle Ned means well, but after the third vino, his capacious details can become excruciatingly painful.

Where will your Ceremony of Life be held?

Again, there are no rules. You can plan to celebrate inside, outside or a combination of both. You can arrange a celebration at the beach that honors your love of the ocean, or at your favorite local pub or place of worship.

Think about the demographics and physical abilities of the people who may be attending. Remember to allow for budgetary considerations around them.

Transportation costs alone may negate your plans for renting that French villa, but the cases of Bordeaux that you can afford in lieu of it, could finally have your nearest and dearest sharing your favourite drink with each other.

Don't expect guests to have to stand for an extended period. They will regrettably, but politely, slide out the door. Select a location with ample seating so that attendees can seek relief as required.

Decor

Simple or elaborate?

- Don't try to incorporate too much into your event. Displaying every special moment, or attempting to deliver what you 'think' people want to see, can be overwhelming for everyone. By focusing on what you love, and keying in on who and what is important to you, you will create an authentic atmosphere where people can relax and celebrate.

- In addition to a photo display, symbols like a senior's favourite chair, a bricklayer's trowel, or a tennis player's racket, can speak a thousand words. Keep it simple.

- You can start doing your part now to make things easier for your organizers. Keep an appropriately sized box accessible. Put anything that you consider to be of significance in it. Include favorite photos, sport jerseys, poems etc. If a box isn't feasible, make a list of items you would consider displaying at your Ceremony of Life and indicate where they can be located.

- Tribute videos can capture everything succinctly yet be very moving. Recording and organizing key memories and accomplishments now, will make future display much easier.

_____

_____

_____

_____

_____

When?

Factors like time of year, location, scheduling, and travel time for attendees may affect when you choose to hold your event. However, you can be as creatively offbeat or as precise with the "when" as you can be with the rest of your planning. You may want to coordinate your event with a sunrise, sunset, or the next full moon.

For sports fans, it may be a matter of getting everyone together to watch the first pitch of the season being thrown out. There is no definitive right or wrong time to hold a celebration.

_____

_____

_____

Activities

If you would like to create a theme or incorporate an activity into your celebration, consider using the following questions to stimulate ideas.

- What do you like most about your life?
  - o _____

- What defines your life? Being of service? Your family? Nature? Fun?
  - o _____

- What do you feel you haven't gotten enough of?
  - o _____

- What final challenge would you like to overcome?
  - o _____

- What would you spend your last dollar on if you had the choice?
  - _____

- What would you do if you knew you had just one more day to do it?
  - _____

Consider the examples below:

- If you want your guests to leave your event laughing, consider including games or focusing around the most amusing aspects of your life. Maybe there is someone you want to play a final joke on, or a puzzle that you want everyone who attends to work on together.

- Extend the spirit of the event with an optional activity that follows. It could be a dance, a game of tag, or a picnic in your favorite park. Plan what would make you happy.

- Arrange the dedication of a park bench, fund training for a seeing eye dog, or establish your own charity.

- Terrified of roller coasters? Instruct the braver among your acquaintances to take you for a ride. Finally conquer that fear!

- Were you ever a collector? Perhaps you have enough of something small to pass out to everyone attending. A conservationist or gardener? Handing out seedlings with instructions for people to plant them randomly may be an option for you.

- Have everyone bring a can of food or a donation for the charity of your choice.

- Into Yoga or Buddhism? Meditate in lieu of prayer or hand out passes to the class you attend.

- Get creative with your ashes. There are companies that can arrange to have your ashes incorporated into fireworks or jewelry, or mixed with paint and used to create pieces of art. Google is a wonderful thing.
- Invite attendees to write a special memory or wish on a small piece of paper. Have the results read out loud during the ceremony or place them in a memory box. Loved ones can refer to them later or ceremoniously bury or burn the box in front of the group.
- Create simple bookmark mementos out of your favourite quote or saying.
- Are you a bibliophile? Invite guests to choose from your collection of books and donate the remainder to local libraries or shelters.
- Announce a pre-set annual reservation for subsequent years – same time, same place – to keep relationships going.
- Share your Mom's recipe for *marshmallow peanut butter squares*.

Food & Refreshments

Breaking bread brings people together.

Refreshments can be incidental or a major focus. If food is

 important to you, what's being served should receive serious consideration during pre-planning.

Taking the following factors into consideration will help to develop a food plan that works.

- Food Budget –continue to add, remove or substitute until it fits
- Crowd Demographics – avoid spicy or gassy foods if your crowd isn't used to them
- Mood of the Celebration – formal or casual
- Sit or Stand? – crowd demographics and food choices can play a major part in planning here
- Favourite Foods – have what you would want to eat
- Location and Amenities – adjust as needed, beach sit-downs can get sandy

Potlucks can make guests feel a part of the event and surpass all expectations when attendees bring dishes that fit a theme, or hold a special meaning.

A licensed event can be topped off by having a bartender create and serve an original drink named after you. Perhaps you already have your own concoction that can be served for the toast. Remember to have both alcoholic and non-alcoholic versions of whatever beverage you choose to serve available. Have a number for a taxi service handy.

_____

_____

_____

_____

_____

Music

- Play what you'd hum.
- Share the music that influenced your life. It will help people feel more connected to you and to each other.
- Provide the words to your favourite songs and have a sing-along if you're into that kind of thing.
- If music wasn't an integral part of your life, having music for at least a portion of the celebration is still a good idea. Quiet background music emits a comforting vibe that can help put people at ease.
- Ask friends for suggestions so everyone can relate to the music.

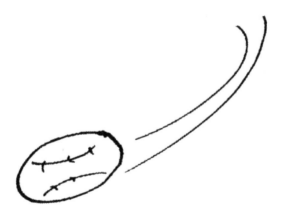

CONGRATULATIONS, YOU'VE GOT YOUR PLAN ...

You've done it. You know the who, the what, the why, when and how, or at the very least have established a rough outline or theme for others to follow should something unexpected happen.

Don't forget to review your plan and have the appropriate friend or relative look over your notes.

File It

Where are you going to keep it? If you haven't already decided, now is the time to make that decision. It can sit alongside your will, in a personal or bank safe, or be physically shared with someone you trust.

Remember, should you decide to make changes, all copies should receive the same adjustments and be signed and dated.

_____

_____

_____

_____

_____

_____

_____

Notes & Observations

Remember, your plan is as alive as you are. If there is something you want changed, change it! If you attend a ceremony and see something you like or dislike, don't rely on your memory. Take notes and keep an ongoing file. Revisit and refine it.

And most importantly, remember, life is short...

... start making more memories *NOW*!

The End ♥.

NOTES:

Printed in the USA
CPSIA information can be obtained
at www.ICGtesting.com
LVHW010213130824
788113LV00009B/469